W9-CFS-055

Silly Snacks

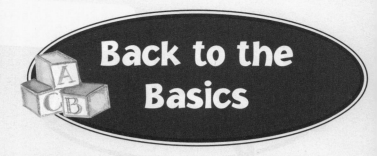

Back to the Basics

Dino-Mite Dinosaurs

   1 cup (2 sticks) butter, softened
1 ¼ cups granulated sugar
   1 large egg
   2 squares (1 ounce each) semi-sweet chocolate, melted
  ½ teaspoon vanilla extract
2 ⅓ cups all-purpose flour
   1 teaspoon baking powder
  ¼ teaspoon salt
   1 cup white frosting
     Assorted food colorings
   1 cup "M&M's"® Chocolate Mini Baking Bits

In large bowl cream butter and sugar until light and fluffy; beat in egg, chocolate and vanilla. In medium bowl combine flour, baking powder and salt; add to creamed mixture; mix well. Wrap and refrigerate dough 2 to 3 hours. Preheat oven to 350°F. Working with half the dough at a time on lightly floured surface, roll to ¼-inch thickness. Cut into dinosaur shapes using 4-inch cookie cutters. Place about 2 inches apart on ungreased cookie sheets. Bake 10 to 12 minutes. Cool 2 minutes on cookie sheets; cool completely on wire racks. Tint frosting desired colors. Frost cookies and decorate with "M&M's"® Chocolate Mini Baking Bits. Store in tightly covered container.   *Makes 2 dozen cookies*

Firecrackers

>   5 cups BAKER'S® ANGEL FLAKE® Coconut
>   Red food coloring
> 24 baked cupcakes, cooled
>   1 tub (12 ounces) COOL WHIP® Whipped Topping,
>   thawed
>   Blue decorating gel
>   Red string licorice

TINT coconut using red food coloring.

TRIM any "lips" off top edges of cupcakes. Using small amount of whipped topping, attach bottoms of 2 cupcakes together. Repeat with remaining cupcakes. Stand attached cupcakes on one end on serving plate or tray.

FROST with remaining whipped topping. Press coconut onto sides.

DRAW a star on top of each firecracker with decorating gel. Insert pieces of licorice for fuses. Store cakes in refrigerator.

Makes 12 Firecrackers

Handprints

1 package (20 ounces) refrigerated cookie dough, any flavor
All-purpose flour (optional)
Cookie glazes, frostings and assorted candies

1. Grease cookie sheets. Remove dough from wrapper according to package directions.

2. Cut dough into 4 equal sections. Reserve 1 section; refrigerate remaining 3 sections. Sprinkle reserved dough with flour to minimize sticking, if necessary.

3. Roll dough on prepared cookie sheet to 5×7-inch rectangle.

4. Place hand, palm-side down, on dough. Carefully, cut around outline of hand with knife. Remove scraps. Separate fingers as much as possible using small spatula. Pat fingers outward to lengthen slightly. Repeat steps with remaining dough.

5. Freeze dough 15 minutes. Preheat oven to 350°F.

6. Bake 7 to 13 minutes or until cookies are set and edges are golden brown. Cool completely on cookie sheets.

7. Decorate as desired.   *Makes 5 adult handprint cookies*

Tip: To get the kids involved, let them use their hands to make the handprints. Be sure that an adult is available to cut around the outline with a knife. The kids will enjoy seeing how their handprints bake into big cookies.

Kaleidoscope Honey Pops

2¼ cups water

¾ cup honey

3 cups assorted fruit, cut into small pieces

12 (3-ounce) paper cups or popsicle molds

12 popsicle sticks

Whisk together water and honey in pitcher until well blended. Place ¼ cup fruit in each mold. Divide honey mixture between cups. Freeze about 1 hour or until partially frozen. Insert popsicle sticks; freeze until firm and ready to serve. *Makes 12 servings*

Favorite recipe from **National Honey Board**

Leapin' Lizards!

1 cup butterscotch-flavor chips

½ cup corn syrup

3 tablespoons butter

1 cup white chocolate chips

Green food color

7 cups crisp rice cereal

Candy corn, green jelly beans, red miniature jaw breakers and chocolate chips

1. Line baking sheet with waxed paper.

2. Combine butterscotch chips, corn syrup and butter in large saucepan. Stir over medium heat until chips are melted. Add white chocolate chips and green food color; stir well. Remove from heat. Add cereal; stir to coat evenly.

3. Lightly butter hands and shape about 1½ cups cereal mixture into lizard (about 6 inches long) as shown in photo. Place on prepared baking sheet. Decorate with candies as shown. Repeat with remaining mixture. *Makes 4 lizards*

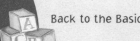
Make Your Own Pizza Shapes

1 package (10 ounces) refrigerated pizza dough
¼ to ½ cup prepared pizza sauce
1 cup shredded mozzarella cheese
1 cup *French's*® French Fried Onions

1. Preheat oven to 425°F. Unroll dough onto greased baking sheet. Press or roll dough into 12×8-inch rectangle. With sharp knife or pizza cutter, cut dough into large shape of your choice (butterfly, heart, star). Reroll scraps and cut into mini shapes. (See tip.)

2. Pre-bake crust 7 minutes or until crust just begins to brown. Spread with sauce and top with cheese. Bake 6 minutes or until crust is deep golden brown.

3. Sprinkle with French Fried Onions. Bake 2 minutes longer or until golden.   *Makes 4 to 6 servings*

Tip: Pizza dough can be cut with 6-inch shaped cookie cutters. Spread with sauce and top with cheese. Bake about 10 minutes or until crust is golden. Sprinkle with French Fried Onions. Bake 2 minutes longer.

Prep Time: 10 minutes
Cook Time: 15 minutes

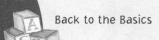

Piggy Wraps

I package HILLSHIRE FARM® Lit'l Smokies
2 cans (8 ounces each) refrigerated crescent roll dough,
cut into small triangles

Preheat oven to 400°F.

Wrap individual Lit'l Smokies in dough triangles. Bake 5 minutes or
until golden brown. *Makes about 50 hors d'oeuvres*

Note: Piggy Wraps may be frozen. To reheat in microwave,
microwave at HIGH 1½ minutes or at MEDIUM-HIGH (70%
power) 2 minutes. When reheated in microwave, dough will not be
crisp.

Quick Pizza Snacks

3 English muffins, split and toasted
I can (14½ ounces) Italian-style diced tomatoes,
undrained
¾ cup (3 ounces) shredded Italian cheese blend
Bell pepper strips (optional)

Preheat oven to 350°F. Place English muffin halves on ungreased
baking sheet. Top each muffin with ¼ cup tomatoes; sprinkle with
2 tablespoons cheese. Bake about 5 minutes or until cheese is
melted and lightly browned. Garnish with bell pepper strips, if
desired. *Makes 6 servings*

Reese's® Haystacks

1⅔ cups (10-ounce package) REESE'S® Peanut Butter
  Chips

1 tablespoon shortening (do *not* use butter, margarine,
  spread or oil)

2½ cups (5-ounce can) chow mein noodles

1. Line tray with wax paper.

2. Place peanut butter chips and shortening in medium
microwave-safe bowl. Microwave at HIGH (100%) 1 minute; stir. If
necessary, microwave at HIGH an additional 15 seconds at a time,
stirring after each heating, just until chips are melted and mixture is
smooth when stirred. Immediately add chow mein noodles; stir to
coat.

3. Drop mixture by heaping teaspoons onto prepared tray or into
paper candy cups. Let stand until firm. If necessary, cover and
refrigerate several minutes until firm. Store in tightly covered
container.   *Makes about 2 dozen treats*

● ● ● ● ● ● ● ● ● ● ●

Why did the cookie
go to the doctor's office?

● ● ● ● ● ● ● ● ● ● ●

Answer: Because he was feeling crummy!

Tic-Tac-Toe Tuna Pizza

>   1 bread-style prepared pizza crust (10 ounces)
>   1 can (12 ounces) tuna packed in water, drained
>   ½ cup minced onion
>   ⅓ cup reduced-fat mayonnaise
>   9 thin plum tomato slices
>   4 to 5 slices (¾ ounce each) process cheese food or
>   American cheese

1. Preheat oven to 425°F. Place bread shell on pizza pan or baking sheet.

2. Combine tuna, onion and mayonnaise in medium bowl; season to taste with salt and pepper. Stir until blended. Spread mixture over bread shell, leaving 1-inch border. Arrange tomato slices on tuna mixture in 3 rows, spacing at least ½ inch apart.

3. Bake 10 to 12 minutes or until heated through.

4. While pizza is baking, cut cheese slices into ½-inch-wide strips.

5. Remove pizza from oven. Arrange enough strips over tuna mixture to resemble tic-tac-toe game. Crisscross remaining strips over some tomato slices. Let stand 5 minutes before serving.

Makes 6 servings

Prep and Cook Time: 30 minutes

Zippity Hot Doggity Tacos

- 1 small onion, finely chopped
- 1 tablespoon *Frank's® RedHot®* Cayenne Pepper Sauce or *French's®* Worcestershire Sauce
- 4 frankfurters, chopped
- 1 can (10½ ounces) red kidney or black beans, drained
- 1 can (8 ounces) tomato sauce
- 1 teaspoon chili powder
- 8 taco shells, heated
- 1 cup *French's®* French Fried Onions
  Garnish: chopped tomatoes, shredded lettuce, sliced olives, sour cream, shredded cheese

1. Heat *1 tablespoon oil* in 12-inch nonstick skillet over medium-high heat. Cook onion, 3 minutes or until crisp-tender. Stir in next five ingredients through chili powder. Bring to boiling. Reduce heat to medium-low and cook 5 minutes, stirring occasionally.

2. To serve, spoon chili into taco shells. Garnish as desired and sprinkle with French Fried Onions. Splash on *Frank's RedHot* Sauce for extra zip!

Makes 4 servings

Prep Time: 5 minutes
Cook Time: 8 minutes

Xippy Cookie Pops

1 package (20 ounces) refrigerated sugar cookie dough
   All-purpose flour (optional)
20 (4-inch) lollipop sticks
   Assorted frostings, glazes and decors

1. Preheat oven to 350°F. Grease cookie sheets.

2. Remove dough from wrapper according to package directions. Sprinkle with flour to minimize sticking, if necessary.

3. Cut dough in half. Reserve 1 half; refrigerate remaining dough. Roll reserved dough to $\frac{1}{8}$-inch thickness. Cut out cookies using $3\frac{1}{2}$-inch cookie cutters.

4. Place lollipop sticks on cookies so that tips of sticks are imbedded in cookies. Carefully turn cookies so sticks are in back; place on prepared cookie sheets. Repeat with remaining dough.

5. Bake 7 to 11 minutes or until edges are lightly browned. Cool cookies on cookie sheets 2 minutes. Remove cookies to wire racks; cool completely.

6. Decorate with frostings, glazes and decors as desired.

Makes 20 cookies

Yummy Frozen Chocolate-Covered Bananas

2 ripe medium bananas
4 wooden sticks
½ cup low-fat granola cereal without raisins
⅓ cup hot fudge sauce, at room temperature

1. Line baking sheet or 15×10-inch jelly-roll pan with waxed paper; set aside.

2. Peel bananas; cut each in half crosswise. Insert wooden stick into center of cut end of each banana about 1½ inches into banana half. Place on prepared baking sheet; freeze until firm, at least 2 hours.

3. Place granola in large plastic food storage bag; crush slightly using rolling pin or meat mallet. Transfer granola to shallow plate. Place fudge sauce in shallow dish.

4. Working with 1 banana at a time, place frozen banana in fudge sauce; turn banana and spread fudge sauce evenly onto banana with small rubber scraper. Immediately place banana on plate with granola; turn to coat lightly. Return to baking sheet in freezer. Repeat with remaining bananas.

5. Freeze until fudge sauce is very firm, at least 2 hours. Place on small plates; let stand 5 minutes before serving.

Makes 4 servings

• • • • • • • • • • • •

What is the difference between a fish and a piano?

• • • • • • • • • • • •

Answer: You can't tuna fish!

Snacks on the Go

Cool Sandwich Snacks

10 whole graham crackers or chocolate-flavor graham
    crackers, cracked in half

½ cup chocolate fudge sauce

1 tub (8 ounces) COOL WHIP® Whipped Topping,
    thawed

Suggested Garnishes: Multi-colored sprinkles, assorted
    candies, finely crushed cookies, chocolate chunks,
    chopped nuts or toasted BAKER'S® ANGEL FLAKE®
    Coconut

SPREAD ½ of the graham crackers lightly with chocolate sauce.
Spread whipped topping about ¾ inch thick on remaining ½ of the
graham crackers. Press crackers together lightly, making sandwiches.
Roll or lightly press edges in suggested garnishes.

FREEZE 4 hours or overnight.   *Makes 10 sandwiches*

Make Ahead: This recipe can be made up to 2 weeks ahead. Wrap
well with plastic wrap and freeze.

Prep Time: 15 minutes
Freeze Time: 4 hours

• • • • • • • • • • • • • •

How do you make a strawberry shake?

• • • • • • • • • • • • • •

Answer: Take it to a scary movie!

Funny Face Sandwich Melts

2 super-size English muffins, split and toasted
8 teaspoons *French's*® Sweet & Tangy Honey Mustard
I can (8 ounces) crushed pineapple, drained
8 ounces sliced smoked ham
4 slices Swiss cheese or white American cheese

I. Place English muffins, cut side up, on baking sheet. Spread each with *2 teaspoons* mustard. Arrange one-fourth of the pineapple, ham and cheese on top, dividing evenly.

2. Broil until cheese melts, about I minute. Decorate with mustard and assorted vegetables to create your own funny face.

Makes 4 servings

Tip: This sandwich is also easy to prepare in the toaster oven.

Prep Time: 10 minutes
Cook Time: I minute

Sugar-and-Spice Twists

I tablespoon sugar
¼ teaspoon ground cinnamon
I package (6) refrigerated breadsticks

I. Preheat oven to 350°F. Lightly grease baking sheet or line with parchment paper.

2. Combine sugar and cinnamon in shallow dish or plate.

3. Open package of breadsticks. Divide into 6 portions. Roll each portion into 12-inch rope. Roll in sugar mixture. Twist into pretzel shape. Place on prepared baking sheet. Bake 15 to 18 minutes or until lightly browned. Remove from baking sheet. Cool 5 minutes. Serve warm.

Makes 6 servings

Tip: Use colored sugar sprinkles in place of the sugar in this recipe for a fun 'twist' of color that's perfect for holidays, birthdays or simply everyday celebrations.

Teddy Bear Party Mix

4 cups crisp cinnamon graham cereal
2 cups honey flavored teddy-shaped graham snacks
1 can (1½ ounces) *French's*® Potato Sticks
3 tablespoons melted unsalted butter
2 tablespoons *French's*® Worcestershire Sauce
1 tablespoon packed brown sugar
¼ teaspoon ground cinnamon
1 cup sweetened dried cranberries or raisins
½ cup chocolate, peanut butter or carob chips

1. Preheat oven to 350°F. Lightly spray jelly-roll pan with nonstick cooking spray. Combine cereal, graham snacks and potato sticks in large bowl.

2. Combine butter, Worcestershire, sugar and cinnamon in small bowl; toss with cereal mixture. Transfer to prepared pan. Bake 12 minutes. Cool completely.

3. Stir in dried cranberries and chips. Store in an air-tight container.   *Makes about 7 cups*

Prep Time: 5 minutes
Cook Time: 12 minutes

• • • • • • • • • • •

**Where is the best place to
see a man-eating fish?**

• • • • • • • • • • •

Answer: In a seafood restaurant!

Easy Cinnamon-Raisin Snails

Snails

> **2 to 3 tablespoons flour**
>
> **1 loaf (16 ounces) frozen bread dough, completely thawed**
>
> **3 tablespoons butter or margarine, divided**
>
> **½ cup packed brown sugar**
>
> **2 teaspoons cinnamon**
>
> **¾ cup SUN-MAID® Raisins or Golden Raisins**

Glaze

> **¼ cup powdered sugar**
>
> **1 to 2 teaspoons milk**

1. **LINE** a baking sheet with aluminum foil for easy clean-up.

2. **SPRINKLE** flour on counter or a large cutting board. Roll dough with a rolling pin on floured surface to an 18×8-inch rectangle.

3. **MELT*** 2 tablespoons butter in a microwave-safe bowl on HIGH for 1 minute. Stir in brown sugar, cinnamon and raisins; sprinkle evenly over dough except on 1 inch along one long side.

4. **ROLL** up dough starting at long sugared side leaving 1 inch free at opposite side.

5. **CUT*** dough into 18 (1-inch-wide) slices. Make the 1-inch ends into "snail heads," by pinching each side and gently pulling out "antennae." Place snails standing upright on baking sheet.

6. **MELT*** 1 tablespoon butter. Use a spoon or pastry brush to coat each snail with butter.

7. **HEAT*** oven to 350°F. Bake snails 18 to 20 minutes or until golden brown.

8. **MAKE GLAZE:** Stir powdered sugar and 1 or 2 teaspoons milk to make a thick glaze. Drizzle glaze over snails. Serve warm.

Makes 18 snails

*Adult supervision is suggested.

Prep Time: 20 minutes
Bake Time: 20 minutes

30

Stuffed Banana Smiles

I **medium size banana, with peel on**
I **tablespoon SUN-MAID® Raisins or Golden Raisins**
I **tablespoon semi-sweet, milk or white chocolate baking chips**

1. **PLACE** banana, with peel on, flat on its side on a microwave-safe plate.

2. **STARTING*** and ending ¼ inch from the ends of banana, cut a slit lengthwise through the banana up to the skin on the other side.

3. **GENTLY** open the banana. Use your fingers to stuff the banana with raisins, then add chocolate chips.

4. **MICROWAVE*** banana uncovered on HIGH for 40 to 60 seconds or until chocolate begins to melt and banana is still firm. Banana skin may darken slightly. Eat immediately, scooping with a spoon right out of the banana peel.   *Makes I serving*

*Adult supervision is suggested.

Tip: At a party, invite guests to prepare their own banana smile!

Tip: On your grill,* place each banana flat on its side, on a piece of aluminum foil and follow steps 2 and 3 above. Wrap bananas loosely and pinch foil closed. Place on covered barbecue grill or over hot coals for about 5 minutes or just until chocolate begins to melt and banana is still firm.

Tip: Place wrapped bananas on a baking sheet and bake in the oven* at 350°F for 5 minutes.

Prep Time: 2 minutes
Bake Time: I minute

Inside-Out Turkey Sandwiches

2 tablespoons fat-free cream cheese
2 tablespoons pasteurized process cheese spread
2 teaspoons chopped green onion tops
1 teaspoon prepared mustard
12 thin round slices fat-free turkey breast or smoked turkey breast
4 large pretzel logs or unsalted breadsticks

1. Combine cream cheese, process cheese spread, green onion and mustard in small bowl; mix well.

2. Arrange 3 turkey slices on large sheet of plastic wrap, overlapping slices in center. Spread 1/4 of cream cheese mixture evenly onto turkey slices, covering slices completely. Place 1 pretzel at bottom edge of turkey slices; roll up turkey around pretzel. (Be sure to keep all 3 turkey slices together as you roll them around pretzel.)

3. Repeat with remaining ingredients.   *Makes 4 servings*

Peanut Butter 'n' Chocolate Chips Snack Mix

6 cups bite-size crisp corn, rice or wheat squares cereal
3 cups miniature pretzels
2 cups toasted oat cereal rings
1 cup raisins or dried fruit bits
1 cup HERSHEY'S Semi-Sweet Chocolate Chips
1 cup REESE'S® Peanut Butter Chips

Stir together all ingredients in large bowl. Store in airtight container at room temperature.   *Makes 14 cups*

Monster Sandwiches

8 assorted round and oblong sandwich rolls
Butter
16 to 24 slices assorted cold cuts (salami, turkey, ham, bologna)
6 to 8 slices assorted cheeses (American, Swiss, Muenster)
1 firm tomato, sliced
1 cucumber, sliced thinly
Assorted lettuce leaves (Romaine, curly, red leaf)
Cocktail onions
Green and black olives
Cherry tomatoes
Pickled gherkins
Radishes
Baby corn
Hard-cooked eggs

1. Cut rolls open just below center and spread with butter.

2. Layer cold cuts, cheeses, tomato and cucumber slices and lettuce leaves to make monster faces. Roll "tongues" from ham slices or make "lips" with tomato slices.

3. Use toothpicks to affix remaining ingredients for eyes, ears, fins, horns, hair, etc.

Makes 8 sandwiches

Super Suggestion!

Remember to remove
toothpicks before eating.

Snacking Surprise Muffins

1½ cups all-purpose flour
1 cup fresh or frozen blueberries
½ cup sugar
2½ teaspoons baking powder
1 teaspoon ground cinnamon
¼ teaspoon salt
⅔ cup buttermilk
1 egg, beaten
¼ cup margarine or butter, melted
3 tablespoons peach preserves

Topping
1 tablespoon sugar
¼ teaspoon ground cinnamon

1. Preheat oven to 400°F. Line 12 medium muffin cups with paper liners; set aside.

2. Combine flour, blueberries, ½ cup sugar, baking powder, 1 teaspoon cinnamon and salt in medium bowl. Combine buttermilk, egg and margarine in small bowl. Add to flour mixture; mix just until moistened.

3. Spoon about 1 tablespoon batter into each muffin cup. Drop a scant teaspoonful of preserves into center of batter in each cup; top with remaining batter.

4. Combine 1 tablespoon sugar and ¼ teaspoon cinnamon in small bowl; sprinkle evenly over tops of batter.

5. Bake 18 to 20 minutes or until lightly browned. Remove muffins to wire rack to cool completely.   *Makes 12 servings*

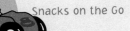

Bologna "Happy Faces"

4 slices whole wheat or rye bread

1 cup prepared oil and vinegar based coleslaw

8 ounces **HEBREW NATIONAL®** Sliced Lean Beef
   Bologna or Lean Beef Salami

4 large pimiento-stuffed green olives
   HEBREW NATIONAL® Deli Mustard

For each sandwich, spread 1 bread slice with 3 tablespoons
coleslaw; top with 5 slices bologna. Cut olives in half crosswise;
place over bologna for "eyes." Draw smiley "mouth" with mustard.
Drop 1 tablespoon coleslaw at top of face for "hair."

Makes 4 open-faced sandwiches

Kool-Pop Treat

1 (3-ounce) bag **ORVILLE REDENBACHER'S®**
   Microwave Popping Corn, popped according to
   package directions

2 cups brightly colored puffed oat cereal, such as fruit
   flavored loops

2 cups miniature marshmallows

1 (.35-ounce) package strawberry soft drink mix

2 tablespoons powdered sugar

1. In large bowl, combine popcorn, cereal and marshmallows.

2. Combine drink mix and powdered sugar; sift over popcorn
mixture. Toss to coat. *Makes 12 (1-cup) servings*

Rock 'n' Rollers

4 (6- to 7-inch) flour tortillas
4 ounces Neufchâtel cheese, softened
⅓ cup peach preserves
1 cup (4 ounces) shredded fat-free Cheddar cheese
½ cup packed washed fresh spinach leaves
3 ounces thinly sliced regular or smoked turkey breast

1. Spread each tortilla evenly with 1 ounce Neufchâtel cheese; cover with thin layer of preserves. Sprinkle with Cheddar cheese.

2. Arrange spinach leaves and turkey over Cheddar cheese. Roll up tortillas; trim ends. Cover and refrigerate until ready to serve.

3. Cut "rollers" crosswise in half or diagonally into 1-inch pieces.

Makes 4 servings

Sassy Salsa Rollers: Substitute salsa for peach preserves and shredded iceberg lettuce for spinach leaves.

Ham 'n' Apple Rollers: Omit peach preserves and spinach leaves. Substitute lean ham slices for turkey. Spread tortillas with Neufchâtel cheese as directed; sprinkle with Cheddar cheese. Top each tortilla with about 2 tablespoons finely chopped apple and 2 ham slices; roll up. Continue as directed.

Wedgies: Prepare Rock 'n' Rollers or any variation as directed, but do not roll up. Top with second tortilla; cut into wedges. Continue as directed.

Jolly Juices & More

Peanut Butter & Jelly Shakes

1 ½ cups vanilla ice cream
¼ cup milk
2 tablespoons creamy peanut butter
6 peanut butter sandwich cookies, coarsely chopped
¼ cup strawberry preserves

1. Place ice cream, milk and peanut butter in blender. Blend on medium speed 1 to 2 minutes or until smooth and well blended. Add cookie pieces and blend 10 seconds on low speed. Pour into 2 serving glasses.

2. Place preserves and 1 to 2 teaspoons water in small bowl; stir until smooth. Stir 2 tablespoons preserve mixture into each glass. Serve immediately.

Makes 2 servings

Serve It With Style!: For a change of pace, prepare these shakes using different flavors of preserves.

Cook's Notes: Eat this thick and creamy shake with a spoon for a mouthful of cookies in every bite.

Prep Time: 10 minutes

"Moo-vin" Chocolate Milk Shakes

    1 pint low-fat sugar-free chocolate ice cream
    ½ cup fat-free (skim) milk
    1 tablespoon chocolate syrup
    ¼ teaspoon vanilla
    ⅛ teaspoon decorator sprinkles (optional)

Combine all ingredients except decorator sprinkles in blender container. Cover and blend until smooth. Pour into 2 small glasses. Add decorator sprinkles, if desired. Serve immediately.

Makes 2 servings

Cherry-Berry Smoothie

    1 cup frozen whole unsweetened pitted dark sweet cherries
    1 cup frozen whole unsweetened strawberries
    1 cup cranberry-cherry juice

In blender, purée frozen pitted dark sweet cherries, frozen strawberries and juice, stirring as needed, until smooth.

Makes 1 (16-ounce) serving

Note: Frozen pitted dark sweet cherries may be replaced with ¾ cup well-drained canned pitted dark sweet cherries and four ice cubes.

Favorite recipe from **National Cherry Growers**

Clockwise from top left: "Moo-vin" Chocolate Milk Shake, "Moo-vin" Vanilla Milk Shake (page 50) and "Moo-vin" Strawberry Milk Shake (page 58)

44

Sparkling Apple Punch

2 bottles (750 mL each) sparkling apple cider, chilled
1½ quarts papaya or apricot nectar, chilled
   Ice
1 or 2 papayas, peeled and chopped
   Orange slices, quartered

Combine apple cider, papaya nectar and ice in punch bowl. Add papaya and orange slices.   *Makes about 4 quarts*

Chocolate Root Beer Float

1 tablespoon sugar
2 teaspoons HERSHEY'S Cocoa
1 tablespoon hot water
1 scoop vanilla ice cream
   Cold root beer

1. Stir together sugar and cocoa in 12-ounce glass; stir in water.

2. Add ice cream and enough root beer to half fill glass; stir gently. Fill glass with root beer. Stir; serve immediately.

Makes one (12-ounce) serving

● ● ● ● ● ● ● ● ● ● ● ● ●

Why did the jelly roll?

● ● ● ● ● ● ● ● ● ● ● ● ●

Answer: Because it saw the apple turnover.

Bottom to top: Sparkling Apple Punch, Citrus Punch (page 49)

Choco-Berry Cooler

¾ cup cold milk

¼ cup sliced fresh strawberries

2 tablespoons HERSHEY'S Syrup

2 tablespoons plus 2 small scoops vanilla ice cream, divided

Cold ginger ale or club soda

Fresh strawberry

Mint leaves (optional)

1. Place milk, strawberries, chocolate syrup and 2 tablespoons ice cream in blender container. Cover and blend until smooth.

2. Alternate remaining 2 scoops of ice cream and chocolate mixture in tall ice cream soda glass; fill glass with ginger ale. Garnish with a fresh strawberry and mint leaves, if desired. Serve immediately.

Makes one (14-ounce) serving

Variations: Before blending, substitute one of the following fruits for fresh strawberries:

• 3 tablespoons frozen strawberries with syrup, thawed

• ½ peeled fresh peach *or* ⅓ cup canned peach slices

• 2 slices canned *or* ¼ cup canned crushed pineapple

• ¼ cup sweetened fresh raspberries *or* 3 tablespoons frozen raspberries with syrup, thawed

Citrus Punch

4 oranges, sectioned
1 to 2 limes, cut into ⅛-inch slices
1 lemon, cut into ⅛-inch slices
1 pint strawberries, stemmed and halved
1 cup raspberries
2 cups orange juice
2 cups grapefruit juice
¾ cup lime juice
½ cup light corn syrup
1 bottle (750 mL) ginger ale or white grape juice
Fresh mint sprigs for garnish

Spread oranges, limes, lemon, strawberries and raspberries on baking sheet. Freeze 4 hours or until firm.

Combine juices and corn syrup in 2-quart pitcher. Stir until corn syrup dissolves. (Stir in additional corn syrup to taste.) Refrigerate 2 hours or until cold. Stir in ginger ale just before serving.

Divide frozen fruit between 8 (12-ounce) glasses or 10 wide-rimmed wine glasses. Fill glasses with punch. Garnish with mint springs, if desired. Serve immediately

Makes 8 to 10 servings (about 5 cups)

Banana Smoothies & Pops

1 (14-ounce) can EAGLE® BRAND Sweetened Condensed Milk (NOT evaporated milk)
1 (8-ounce) container vanilla yogurt
2 ripe bananas
½ cup orange juice

1. In blender container, combine all ingredients; blend until smooth. Stop occasionally to scrape down sides.

2. Serve immediately. Store leftovers covered in refrigerator.

Makes 4 cups

Banana Smoothie Pops: Spoon banana mixture into 8 (5-ounce) paper cups. Freeze 30 minutes. Insert wooden craft sticks into the center of each cup; freeze until firm. Makes 8 pops.

Fruit Smoothies: Substitute 1 cup of your favorite fruit and ½ cup any fruit juice for bananas and orange juice.

Prep Time: 5 minutes

"Moo-vin" Vanilla Milk Shakes

1 pint low-fat sugar-free vanilla ice cream
½ cup fat-free (skim) milk
½ teaspoon vanilla
⅛ teaspoon decorator sprinkles (optional)

Combine all ingredients except decorator sprinkles in blender container. Cover and blend until smooth. Pour into 2 small glasses. Add decorator sprinkles, if desired. Serve immediately.

Makes 2 servings

Bobbing Head Punch

Assorted candies
Assorted fruit slices and pieces
Water
6 cups white grape juice
2 cups apple juice or 2 additional cups ginger ale
4 cups ginger ale
Green food coloring

1. Arrange candies and fruit pieces in bottom of 9-inch glass pie plate to create a face. (Remember, the bottom of the face is what will show in the punch bowl.)

2. Add water to cover face and carefully place in freezer. Freeze overnight.

3. At time of serving, add juices and ginger ale to 4- to 5-quart punch bowl. Tint mixture green. Invert pie plate, placing one hand underneath, and run under cold running water to release frozen face. Place ice mold upside down on top of juice mixture and serve.

Makes 20 cups

Plum Slush

6 fresh California plums, halved, pitted and coarsely
   chopped
1 can (6 ounces) frozen cranberry juice concentrate
20 ice cubes, cracked

Add plums, juice concentrate and ice cubes to food processor or blender. Process until smooth. Serve immediately.

Makes 8 servings

Favorite recipe from **California Tree Fruit Agreement**

Purple Cow Jumped Over the Moon

3 cups vanilla nonfat frozen yogurt

1 cup reduced-fat (2%) milk

½ cup thawed frozen grape juice concentrate (undiluted)

1½ teaspoons lemon juice

Place yogurt, milk, grape juice concentrate and lemon juice in food processor or blender container; process until smooth. Serve immediately.   *Makes 8 (½-cup) servings*

Razzmatazz Shake: Place 1 quart vanilla nonfat frozen yogurt, 1 cup vanilla nonfat yogurt and ¼ cup chocolate nonfat syrup in food processor or blender container; process until smooth. Pour ½ of mixture evenly into 12 glasses; top with ½ of (12-ounce) can root beer. Fill glasses equally with remaining yogurt mixture; top with remaining root beer. Makes 12 (⅔-cup) servings.

Sunshine Shake: Place 1 quart vanilla nonfat frozen yogurt, 1⅓ cups orange juice, 1 cup fresh or thawed frozen raspberries and 1 teaspoon sugar in food processor or blender container; process until smooth. Pour into 10 glasses; sprinkle with ground nutmeg. Makes 10 (½-cup) servings.

Fruit 'n Juice Breakfast Shake

1 extra-ripe, medium DOLE® Banana

¾ cup DOLE® Pineapple Juice

½ cup lowfat vanilla yogurt

½ cup blueberries

Combine all ingredients in blender. Blend until smooth.

Makes 2 servings

Shamrock Smoothies

1 tablespoon sugar

2 green spearmint candy leaves

2 thin round chocolate mints or chocolate sandwich cookies

1 ripe banana, peeled and cut into chunks

1 cup ice cubes

¾ cup apple juice

¼ cup plain yogurt

½ teaspoon vanilla

¼ teaspoon orange extract

2 or 3 drops green food color

1. Place small sheet of waxed paper on work surface; sprinkle with sugar. Place spearmint leaves on waxed paper; top with second sheet of waxed paper. Roll out leaves to ¼-inch thickness. Cut out 2 (1¼×1-inch) shamrock shapes using small knife or scissors. Press 1 shamrock onto each mint; set aside.

2. Place banana, ice cubes, apple juice, yogurt, vanilla, orange extract and food color in blender or food processor; blend until smooth and frothy. Pour into glasses. Garnish with mints.

Makes 2 servings (about 8 ounces each)

Easy Pudding Milk Shake

3 cups cold milk

I package (4-serving size) JELL-O® Instant Pudding &
    Pie Filling, any flavor

1½ cups ice cream, any flavor

POUR milk into blender container. Add pudding mix and ice
cream; cover. Blend on high speed 30 seconds or until smooth. Pour
into glasses and garnish as desired. Serve immediately.

Makes 5 servings

Prep Time: 5 minutes

"Moo-vin" Strawberry Milk Shakes

I pint low-fat sugar-free vanilla ice cream

I cup thawed frozen unsweetened strawberries

¼ cup fat-free (skim) milk

¼ teaspoon vanilla

Combine all ingredients in blender container. Cover and blend until
smooth. Pour into 2 small glasses. Serve immediately.

Makes 2 servings

Monkey Shake

2 cups cold milk

I ripe banana

I package (4-serving size) JELL-O® Chocolate Flavor
Instant Pudding & Pie Filling

2 cups crushed ice

POUR milk into blender container. Add banana, pudding mix and ice; cover. Blend on high speed 15 seconds or until smooth. Serve at once.

Makes 4 servings

How To: Mixture will thicken as it stands. To thin, just add more milk, 1/4 cup at a time for desired thickness.

Great Substitute: Try using JELL-O® White Chocolate Flavor Instant Pudding instead of Chocolate Flavor.

Prep Time: 10 minutes

Cookie Milk Shakes

I pint vanilla ice cream

4 chocolate sandwich cookies or chocolate-covered
graham crackers

Scoop ice cream into blender fitted with metal blade. Crush cookies in resealable plastic food storage bag with rolling pin or in food processor. Place cookies in blender. Process until well-combined. Pour into 2 glasses. Serve immediately.

Makes 2 milk shakes

"Moo-vin" Chocolate-Cherry Milk Shakes

　1 pint low-fat sugar-free chocolate ice cream
　¾ cup drained canned pitted tart red cherries
　¼ cup fat-free (skim) milk
　¼ teaspoon vanilla
　⅛ teaspoon decorator sprinkles (optional)

Combine all ingredients except decorator sprinkles in blender container. Cover and blend until smooth. Pour into 2 small glasses. Add decorator sprinkles, if desired. Serve immediately.

Makes 2 servings

Strawberry Lemonade

　1 cup fresh strawberries, quartered
　1 cup fresh lemon juice (from about 4 lemons)
　¾ cup sucralose, granular form*
　4 cups water

Sold as SPLENDA®

1. Place strawberries in food processor or blender; process until smooth. Pour into large pitcher.

2. Add lemon juice to pitcher along with sucralose and water. Stir.

3. Strain strawberry seeds and pulp, if desired, by pouring lemonade through strainer.

4. Serve in tall glasses filled with ice.

Makes 4 servings

Surprise Package Cupcakes

I package (18 ounces) chocolate cake mix, plus ingredients to prepare mix

Food coloring (optional)

I can (16 ounces) vanilla frosting

I tube (4¼ ounces) white decorator icing

72 chewy fruit squares, assorted colors

Assorted round sprinkles and birthday candles

1. Line standard (2½-inch) muffin cups with paper liners, or spray with nonstick cooking spray. Prepare cake mix and bake in muffin cups according to directions. Cool in pans on wire racks 15 minutes. Remove cupcakes and cool completely.

2. If desired, tint frosting with food coloring, adding a few drops at a time until desired color is reached. Frost cupcakes with white or tinted frosting.

3. Use decorator icing to pipe "ribbons" on fruit squares to resemble wrapped presents. Place 3 candy presents on each cupcake. Decorate with sprinkles and candles as desired.

Makes 24 cupcakes

Corn Dogs

- 8 hot dogs
- 8 wooden craft sticks
- 1 package (about 16 ounces) refrigerated grand-size corn biscuits
- 1/3 cup *French's*® Classic Yellow® Mustard
- 8 slices American cheese, cut in half

1. Preheat oven to 350°F. Insert 1 wooden craft stick halfway into each hot dog; set aside.

2. Separate biscuits. On floured board, press or roll each biscuit into a 7×4-inch oval. Spread *2 teaspoons* mustard lengthwise down center of each biscuit. Top each with 2 pieces of cheese. Place hot dog in center of biscuit. Fold top of dough over end of hot dog. Fold sides towards center enclosing hot dog. Pinch edges to seal.

3. Place corn dogs, seam-side down, on greased baking sheet. Bake 20 to 25 minutes or until golden brown. Cool slightly before serving.

Makes 8 servings

Tip: Corn dogs may be made without wooden craft sticks.

Prep Time: 15 minutes
Cook Time: 20 minutes

Cartoona Sandwiches

1/2 cup low fat mayonnaise

1/2 cup plain low fat yogurt

1 1/2 teaspoons curry powder (optional)

1 cup **SUN-MAID®** Raisins or Fruit Bits

1/2 cup diced celery, or red or green bell pepper

1 green onion, thinly sliced

1 large can (12 ounces) tuna packed in water, or substitute 1 1/4 cups chopped cooked chicken (two small chicken breasts)

6 sandwich rolls, round or oblong shaped

1. **MAKE FILLING:** Mix in a medium bowl, the mayonnaise, yogurt, curry powder, if desired, Sun-Maid® Raisins or Fruit Bits, celery or bell pepper, and green onion. Stir in tuna or chicken.

2. **MAKE "CAR":** Cut* a 1/2-inch slice off the top of a roll. With fingers or a fork, scoop out bread from center of roll.

3. **ATTACH** Sun-Maid® Apricots, carrot slices or other round ingredient to a toothpick to make car "wheels." Insert wheels into bottom edge of roll. Add apple slices for "fenders," if desired.

4. **MAKE** "headlights" using toothpicks to attach raisins on one end of the roll. Cut "doors" in sides of roll, if desired.

5. **FILL** roll with about 1/2 cup tuna or chicken salad. Place roll top on top of "car." Repeat with remaining rolls. Remove all toothpicks before eating. *Makes 6 sandwiches*

*Adult supervision is suggested.

Prep Time: 20 minutes

Cookies & Cream Cupcakes

2¼ cups all-purpose flour

1 tablespoon baking powder

½ teaspoon salt

1⅔ cups sugar

½ cup (1 stick) butter, softened

1 cup milk

2 teaspoons vanilla

3 egg whites

1 cup crushed chocolate sandwich cookies (about 10 cookies) plus additional for garnish

1 container (16 ounces) vanilla frosting

1. Preheat oven to 350°F. Line 24 standard (2½-inch) muffin pan cups with paper liners.

2. Sift flour, baking powder and salt together in large bowl. Stir in sugar. Add butter, milk and vanilla; beat with electric mixer at low speed 30 seconds. Beat at medium speed 2 minutes. Add egg whites; beat 2 minutes. Stir in 1 cup crushed cookies.

3. Spoon batter into prepared muffin pans. Bake 20 to 25 minutes or until toothpick inserted into centers comes out clean. Cool in pans on wire racks 10 minutes. Remove to racks; cool completely.

4. Frost cupcakes; garnish with additional crushed cookies.

Makes 24 cupcakes

Baseball Sandwich

Ingredients

- 1 (1-pound) round sourdough or white bread loaf
- 2 cups mayonnaise or salad dressing, divided
- ¼ pound thinly sliced roast beef
- 1 slice (about 1 ounce) provolone or Swiss cheese
- 3 tablespoons roasted red peppers, well drained
- 3 tablespoons spicy mustard, divided
- ¼ pound thinly sliced ham
- 1 slice (about 1 ounce) Cheddar cheese
- 3 tablespoons dill pickle slices
- 2 tablespoons thinly sliced onion
- Red food color

Supplies

Pastry bag and small writing tip

1. Cut thin slice off top of bread loaf; set aside. With serrated knife, cut around sides of bread, leaving ¼-inch-thick bread shell. Lift out center portion of bread; horizontally cut removed bread round into 3 slices of equal thickness.

2. Spread 1 tablespoon mayonnaise onto bottom of hollowed out loaf; top with layers of roast beef and provolone cheese. Cover with bottom bread slice and red peppers.

3. Spread top of middle bread slice with ½ of mustard; place over peppers. Top with layers of ham and Cheddar cheese. Spread remaining bread slice with remaining mustard; place over ham and Cheddar cheese. Top with pickles and onion. Replace top of bread loaf.

4. Reserve ⅓ cup mayonnaise; set aside. Frost outside of entire loaf of bread with remaining mayonnaise. Color reserved ⅓ cup mayonnaise with red food color; spoon into pastry bag fitted with writing tip. Pipe red mayonnaise onto bread to resemble stitches on baseball. *Makes 6 to 8 servings*

S'Mores on a Stick

1 (14-ounce) can EAGLE® BRAND Sweetened Condensed Milk (NOT evaporated milk), divided

1½ cups milk chocolate mini chips, divided

1 cup miniature marshmallows

11 whole graham crackers, halved crosswise

Toppings: chopped peanuts, mini candy-coated chocolate pieces, sprinkles

1. Microwave half of Eagle Brand in microwave-safe bowl at HIGH (100% power) 1½ minutes. Stir in 1 cup chips until smooth; stir in marshmallows.

2. Spread evenly by heaping tablespoonfuls onto 11 graham cracker halves. Top with remaining graham cracker halves; place on waxed paper.

3. Microwave remaining Eagle Brand at HIGH (100% power) 1½ minutes; stir in remaining ½ cup chips, stirring until smooth. Drizzle mixture over cookies and sprinkle with desired toppings.

4. Let stand for 2 hours; insert a wooden craft stick into center of each cookie. *Makes 11 servings*

Prep Time: 10 minutes
Cook Time: 3 minutes

Lazy Daisy Cupcakes

    1 package (18 ounces) yellow cake mix, plus ingredients
        to prepare mix
    Food coloring
    1 can (16 ounces) vanilla frosting
    30 large marshmallows
    24 small round candies or gum drops

1. Line standard (2½-inch) muffin cups with paper liners, or spray with nonstick cooking spray. Prepare cake and bake in muffin cups according to directions. Cool in pans on wire racks 15 minutes. Remove cupcakes and cool completely.

2. Add food coloring to frosting, a few drops at a time, until desired color is reached. Frost cooled cupcakes with tinted frosting.

3. With scissors, cut each marshmallow crosswise into 4 pieces. Stretch pieces into petal shapes and place 5 pieces on each cupcake to form a flower. Place candy in center of each flower.

Makes 24 cupcakes

● ● ● ● ● ● ● ● ● ● ● ●

Why did the strawberry need a lawyer?

● ● ● ● ● ● ● ● ● ● ● ●

Answer: Because it was in a jam!

Cool Candy Cones

6 flat-bottom ice cream cones

1 tub (8 ounces) **COOL WHIP®** Whipped Topping, thawed

⅓ cup multicolored sprinkles

1 cup chopped candy bars (chocolate-covered wafer bars, peanut butter cups, etc.)

SPREAD top rims of ice cream cones with whipped topping. Roll in sprinkles.

STIR candy into remaining topping. Carefully spoon into prepared ice cream cones. Garnish tops with additional chopped candy and sprinkles, if desired. Serve immediately, or refrigerate or freeze until ready to serve. *Makes 6 servings*

Berries and Cream: Substitute 1 cup raspberries or chopped strawberries for the chopped candy bars.

Prep Time: 10 minutes

Aquarium Cups

¾ cup boiling water

1 package (4-serving size) **JELL-O®** Brand Berry Blue Flavor Gelatin Dessert

½ cup cold water

Ice cubes

Gummy fish

STIR boiling water into gelatin in medium bowl at least 2 minutes until completely dissolved. Mix cold water and ice cubes to make 1¼ cups. Add to gelatin, stirring until slightly thickened. Remove any remaining ice. (If mixture is still thin, refrigerate until slightly thickened.)

POUR thickened gelatin into 4 dessert dishes. Suspend gummy fish in gelatin. Refrigerate 1 hour or until firm. *Makes 4 servings*

Prep Time: 10 minutes
Chill Time: 1 hour

Cool Candy Cones

Colorific Pizza Cookie

   1 package (17½ ounces) sugar cookie mix
   ⅔ cup mini candy-coated chocolate pieces
   ⅓ cup powdered sugar
   2 to 3 teaspoons milk

Preheat oven to 375°F.

Prepare cookie mix according to package directions. Spread into ungreased 12-inch pizza pan. Sprinkle evenly with chocolate pieces; press gently into dough.

Bake 20 to 24 minutes or until lightly browned. Cool 2 minutes in pan. Transfer to wire rack and cool completely.

Blend powdered sugar and milk until smooth, adding enough milk to reach drizzling consistency. Drizzle icing over cooled pizza cookie with spoon or fork. Cut into wedges. *Makes 12 servings*

Hershey's Syrup Snacking Brownies

   ½ cup (1 stick) butter or margarine, softened
   1 cup sugar
   1½ cups (16-ounce can) HERSHEY'S Syrup
   4 eggs
   1¼ cups all-purpose flour
   1 cup HERSHEY'S Semi-Sweet Chocolate Chips

1. Heat oven to 350°F. Grease 13×9×2-inch baking pan.

2. Beat butter and sugar in large bowl. Add syrup, eggs and flour; beat well. Stir in chocolate chips. Pour batter into prepared pan.

3. Bake 30 to 35 minutes or until brownies begin to pull away from sides of pan. Cool completely in pan on wire rack. Cut into bars. *Makes about 36 brownies*

Cookie Pizza

- 1 (18-ounce) package refrigerated sugar cookie dough
- 2 cups (12 ounces) semi-sweet chocolate chips
- 1 (14-ounce) can **EAGLE® BRAND** Sweetened Condensed Milk (**NOT** evaporated milk)
- 2 cups candy-coated milk chocolate candies
- 2 cups miniature marshmallows
- ½ cup peanuts

1. Preheat oven to 375°F. Press cookie dough into 2 ungreased 12-inch pizza pans. Bake 10 minutes or until golden. Remove from oven.

2. In medium-sized saucepan, melt chips with Eagle Brand. Spread over crusts. Sprinkle with milk chocolate candies, marshmallows and peanuts.

3. Bake 4 minutes or until marshmallows are lightly toasted. Cool. Cut into wedges.

Makes 2 pizzas (24 servings)

Prep Time: 15 minutes
Bake Time: 14 minutes

**What did the baby corn
say to the mommy corn?**

Answer: Where's pop corn?

Magical Marshmallow Carpets

- **1 package (8-serving size)** *or* **2 packages (4-serving size each) JELL-O® Brand Gelatin, any flavor**
- **1 cup warm water**
- **3 cups JET-PUFFED® Miniature Marshmallows** *or* **12 JET-PUFFED® Marshmallows**

LIGHTLY GREASE 13×9-inch baking pan with no stick cooking spray.

STIR gelatin and water in medium microwavable bowl. Microwave on HIGH 2½ minutes; stir until dissolved.

STIR in marshmallows. Microwave on HIGH 2 minutes or until marshmallows are partially melted. Stir mixture slowly until marshmallows are completely melted. Pour mixture into pan.

REFRIGERATE 1 hour or until set. Cut gelatin into 2¼×4¼-inch rectangles. With marshmallow layer on top, cut small slits on each side of the rectangles to form "carpet fringes." Garnish each "carpet" with multicolored sprinkles, if desired.

Makes 16 pieces

Variation: To make JELL-O® Marshmallow JIGGLERS®, do not cut into rectangles. Cut out shapes with 1-inch metal cookie cutters. For 2-color JIGGLERS®, prepare recipe as directed above. After refrigerating, repeat recipe in same pan with another gelatin flavor. Cut out shapes.

Prep Time: 10 minutes plus refrigerating

Chocolate-Caramel S'Mores

12 chocolate wafer cookies or chocolate graham cracker
   squares
2 tablespoons fat-free caramel topping
6 large marshmallows

1. Prepare coals for grilling. Place 6 wafer cookies top-down on
plate. Spread 1 teaspoon caramel topping in center of each wafer to
within about ¼ inch of edge.

2. Spear 1 to 2 marshmallows onto long wood-handled skewer.*
Hold several inches above coals 3 to 5 minutes or until
marshmallows are golden and very soft, turning slowly. Push
1 marshmallow off into center of caramel. Top with plain wafer.
Repeat with remaining marshmallows and wafers.

Makes 6 servings

If wood-handled skewers are unavailable, use oven mitt to protect hand from heat.

Note: S'mores, a favorite campfire treat, got their name because
everyone who tasted them wanted "some more." In the unlikely
event of leftover S'mores, they can be reheated in the microwave at
HIGH 15 to 30 seconds.

Funny Face Cookies

4 large cookies (about 4 inches in diameter)
½ cup thawed COOL WHIP® Whipped Topping
   Assorted candies and sprinkles
   BAKER'S® Semi-Sweet Real Chocolate Chunks
   Toasted BAKER'S ANGEL FLAKE® Coconut

SPREAD each cookie with about 2 tablespoons of the whipped
topping.

DECORATE with candies, sprinkles, chunks and coconut to
resemble faces. Serve immediately.

Makes 4 servings

"Everything but the Kitchen Sink" Bar Cookies

1 package (18 ounces) refrigerated chocolate chip
    cookie dough
1 jar (7 ounces) marshmallow creme
½ cup creamy peanut butter
1½ cups toasted corn cereal
½ cup miniature candy-coated chocolate pieces

1. Preheat oven to 350°F. Grease 13×9-inch baking pan. Remove dough from wrapper according to package directions.

2. Press dough into prepared baking pan. Bake 13 minutes.

3. Remove baking pan from oven. Drop teaspoonfuls of marshmallow creme and peanut butter over hot cookie base.

4. Bake 1 minute. Carefully spread marshmallow creme and peanut butter over cookie base.

5. Sprinkle cereal and chocolate pieces over melted marshmallow and peanut butter mixture.

6. Bake 7 minutes. Cool completely on wire rack. Cut into 2-inch bars.

Makes 3 dozen bars

Super Suggestion!

Experiment with this recipe using your favorite candies. Try substituting peanut butter chips in place of chocolate pieces.

Mice Creams

I pint vanilla ice cream

1 (4-ounce) package **READY CRUST®** Mini-Graham Cracker Pie Crusts

Ears—12 KEEBLER® Grasshopper® cookies

Tails—3 chocolate twigs, broken in half *or* 6 (3-inch) pieces black shoestring licorice

Eyes and noses—18 brown candy-coated chocolate candies

Whiskers—2 teaspoons chocolate sprinkles

Place I scoop vanilla ice cream into each crust. Press cookie ears and tails into ice cream. Press eyes, noses and whiskers in place. Serve immediately. Do not refreeze.   *Makes 6 servings*

Prep Time: 15 minutes

Polar Bear Banana Bites

I medium banana, cut into 6 equal-size pieces

¼ cup creamy peanut butter*

3 tablespoons fat-free (skim) milk

¼ cup miniature-size marshmallows

2 tablespoons unsalted dry-roasted peanuts, chopped

I tablespoon chocolate-flavored decorator sprinkles

Soy butter or almond butter can be used in place of peanut butter.

1. Insert wooden pick into each banana piece. Place on tray lined with waxed paper.

2. Whisk together peanut butter and milk. Combine marshmallows, peanuts and chocolate sprinkles in shallow dish. Dip each banana piece in peanut butter mixture, draining off excess. Roll in peanut mixture. Place on tray; let stand until set.

Makes 3 servings

Frozen Berry Ice Cream

8 ounces frozen unsweetened strawberries, partially
thawed

8 ounces frozen unsweetened peaches, partially thawed

4 ounces frozen unsweetened blueberries, partially
thawed

6 packets sugar substitute

2 teaspoons vanilla

2 cups no-sugar-added light vanilla ice cream

16 blueberries

4 small strawberries, halved

8 peach slices

1. In food processor, combine frozen strawberries, peaches,
blueberries, sugar substitute and vanilla. Process until coarsely
chopped.

2. Add ice cream; process until well blended.

3. Serve immediately for semi-soft texture or freeze until needed
and allow to stand 10 minutes to soften slightly. Garnish each
serving with 2 blueberries for "eyes," 1 strawberry half for "nose"
and 1 peach slice for "smile."   *Makes 8 servings (¹/₂ cup each)*

Cookies and Creme Snacks

1 cup chocolate sandwich cookie crumbs *or* chocolate
wafer cookie crumbs

1 tub (8 ounces) COOL WHIP® Whipped Topping,
thawed

STIR cookie crumbs into whipped topping. Spoon into snack cups
or flat-bottom ice cream cones.

REFRIGERATE or freeze until ready to serve.

Makes 6 to 8 servings

Prep Time: 5 minutes

Bamboozlers

 1 cup all-purpose flour
 ¾ cup packed light brown sugar
 ¼ cup unsweetened cocoa powder
 1 egg
 2 egg whites
 5 tablespoons margarine, melted
 ¼ cup fat-free (skim) milk
 ¼ cup honey
 1 teaspoon vanilla
 2 tablespoons semisweet chocolate chips
 2 tablespoons coarsely chopped walnuts
 Powdered sugar (optional)

1. Preheat oven to 350°F. Grease and flour 8-inch square baking pan; set aside.

2. Combine flour, brown sugar and cocoa in medium bowl. Blend together egg, egg whites, margarine, milk, honey and vanilla in medium bowl. Add to flour mixture; mix well. Pour into prepared baking pan; sprinkle with chocolate chips and walnuts.

3. Bake brownies until they spring back when lightly touched in center, about 30 minutes. Cool completely in pan on wire rack. Sprinkle with powdered sugar just before serving, if desired.

Makes 1 dozen brownies

Peanutters: Substitute peanut butter chips for chocolate chips and peanuts for walnuts.

Butterscotch Babies: Substitute butterscotch chips for chocolate chips and pecans for walnuts.

Brownie Sundaes: Serve brownies on dessert plates. Top each brownie with a scoop of vanilla nonfat frozen yogurt and 2 tablespoons nonfat chocolate or caramel sauce.

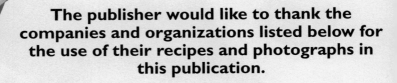

The publisher would like to thank the companies and organizations listed below for the use of their recipes and photographs in this publication.

Birds Eye®

California Tree Fruit Agreement

ConAgra Foods®

Dole Food Company, Inc.

Eagle Brand®

Hebrew National®

Hershey Foods Corporation

Hillshire Farm®

JOLLY TIME® Pop Corn

Keebler® Company

Kraft Foods Holdings

Lawry's® Foods

© Mars, Incorporated 2004

National Cherry Growers & Industries Foundation

National Honey Board

Peanut Advisory Board

Reckitt Benckiser Inc.

The J.M. Smucker Company

Sun•Maid® Growers of California

METRIC CONVERSION CHART

VOLUME MEASUREMENTS (dry)

⅛ teaspoon = 0.5 mL
¼ teaspoon = 1 mL
½ teaspoon = 2 mL
¾ teaspoon = 4 mL
1 teaspoon = 5 mL
1 tablespoon = 15 mL
2 tablespoons = 30 mL
¼ cup = 60 mL
⅓ cup = 75 mL
½ cup = 125 mL
⅔ cup = 150 mL
¾ cup = 175 mL
1 cup = 250 mL
2 cups = 1 pint = 500 mL
3 cups = 750 mL
4 cups = 1 quart = 1 L

VOLUME MEASUREMENTS (fluid)

1 fluid ounce (2 tablespoons) = 30 mL
4 fluid ounces (½ cup) = 125 mL
8 fluid ounces (1 cup) = 250 mL
12 fluid ounces (1½ cups) = 375 mL
16 fluid ounces (2 cups) = 500 mL

WEIGHTS (mass)

½ ounce = 15 g
1 ounce = 30 g
3 ounces = 90 g
4 ounces = 120 g
8 ounces = 225 g
10 ounces = 285 g
12 ounces = 360 g
16 ounces = 1 pound = 450 g

DIMENSIONS

1/16 inch = 2 mm
⅛ inch = 3 mm
¼ inch = 6 mm
½ inch = 1.5 cm
¾ inch = 2 cm
1 inch = 2.5 cm

OVEN TEMPERATURES

250°F = 120°C
275°F = 140°C
300°F = 150°C
325°F = 160°C
350°F = 180°C
375°F = 190°C
400°F = 200°C
425°F = 220°C
450°F = 230°C

BAKING PAN SIZES

Utensil	Size in Inches/Quarts	Metric Volume	Size in Centimeters
Baking or Cake Pan (square or rectangular)	8×8×2	2 L	20×20×5
	9×9×2	2.5 L	23×23×5
	12×8×2	3 L	30×20×5
	13×9×2	3.5 L	33×23×5
Loaf Pan	8×4×3	1.5 L	20×10×7
	9×5×3	2 L	23×13×7
Round Layer Cake Pan	8×1½	1.2 L	20×4
	9×1½	1.5 L	23×4
Pie Plate	8×1¼	750 mL	20×3
	9×1¼	1 L	23×3
Baking Dish or Casserole	1 quart	1 L	—
	1½ quart	1.5 L	—
	2 quart	2 L	—

Can you imagine your children eating fruits and vegetables? They will now when you make them these bizarre, funny, out-of-this-world, tasty treats from Silly Snacks. Snacks like Monster Sandwiches and Funny Face Sandwich Melts will disappear as fast as our Cool Candy Cones and Choco-Berry Cooler. Your kids will be giggling all the way to a clean plate!

Manufactured in China.

ISBN-13: 978-1-4127-0638-4
ISBN-10: 1-4127-0638-6

Publications International, Ltd.
Lincolnwood, IL 60712

50800

9 781412 706384

EAN

0 42799 70638 1

UPC

Silly Snacks

Discover more of your favorite recipes!

For additional titles write to:

Favorite All Time Recipes™
7373 N. Cicero Ave.
Lincolnwood, IL 60712

Pictured on the front cover: Mice Creams *(page 86)*.

Pictured on the back cover *(clockwise from top left):* Zippity Hot Doggity Tacos *(page 18),* Cool Sandwich Snacks *(page 24)* and Dino-Mite Dinosaur *(page 2).*

Microwave Cooking: Microwave ovens vary in wattage. Use the cooking times as guidelines and check for doneness before adding more time.

Preparation/Cooking Times: Preparation times are based on the approximate amount of time required to assemble the recipe before cooking, baking, chilling or serving. These times include preparation steps such as measuring, chopping and mixing. The fact that some preparations and cooking can be done simultaneously is taken into account. Preparation of optional ingredients and serving suggestions is not included.

Publications International, Ltd.